C...,

Dad,
Thank you
for being.

Rene

From the four directions, rain clouds
appear with lightning and
thunder reverberating over the
land, bringing gentle rain. The
land bursts forth in bloom and
animals romp happily in the
green fields. Thus they celebrate
their being, their becoming,
and the fullness of life.

—*from a Hopi kachina song*

A Celebration of Being

A Celebration of Being

PHOTOGRAPHS OF THE HOPI AND NAVAJO

by Susanne Page
Foreword by Robert Redford
Afterword by Jake Page

Northland Publishing

For my parents,
Virginia and Frank Stone, with love,
and of course for Jake, husband, friend,
and irrepressible troublemaker.

SPECIAL EDITION

Designed by David Jenney
Composed in the United States of America
Printed in Japan by Dai Nippon

Library of Congress
Cataloging-in-Publication Data

Page, Susanne.
        A celebration of being: photographs of the Hopi
    and Navajo/by Susanne Page; foreword by Robert
    Redford; afterword by Jake Page. —1st ed.
            p.   cm.
        ISBN 0-87358-495-3 (soft): $24.95
        1. Hopi Indians—Pictorial works.
    2. Navajo Indians—Pictorial works.
    3. Hopi Indians.   4. Navajo Indians.   I. Title.
    E99.H7P3 1989
    973′.04972—dc20   89-42664
                                                    CIP

CONTENTS

FOREWORD

My initial draw to Indian country was unfathomable. I was taken there as a child and had no family or historical frame of reference of any kind. But there it was—undeniable and magnetic. And since that first visit I have remained fascinated and absorbed. In the lands of the Hopi and Navajo, I feel the special splendor of the earth and return again and again to find the peacefulness unique to that geography. In the friendships I have been lucky enough to have formed among the people of these lands, I have found humor, warmth, and a wisdom and spirituality that are both inspiring and sustaining.

In a period when the dominant cultures of the world find themselves wittingly and unwittingly engaged in savaging nature and are under the gun to find new philosophies of restraint, there is much we can learn from the people so beautifully represented in this book. It boils down to an old idea many of us have forgotten: we are not observers or overlords of nature, we are part of nature as truly as an eagle is, or a windstorm. In these Indian lands, I am always refreshed, and recharged with the notion that our lives and spirit are the gifts of nature and that we are obliged to reciprocate. Often, through good fortune, I have been a guest in Hopi and Navajo homes,

and am reminded that we are all guests on the earth, not its landlords.

In the faces of the people who dwell here, I see a special kind of hope—the hope that arises from a certain knowledge of one's place in nature—and I am reminded that the strength of our society as a whole lies in the vigor of its many angles of view, its diversity and tolerance. These ancient lifeways—Navajo and Hopi—and their continuing richness are priceless jewels, crucial elements in our own self-esteem. The dancing dark eyes of these children gleam with all of our futures.

That is the spirit of this book. It arose from an exhibition of photographs that has appeared in several museums and galleries in the nation, and that I was happy to bring to the Sundance Institute in the winter of 1988. More than that, it arose from two decades of dedicated work among the two tribes by Susanne Page, a rare photographer whose eye is guided by her heart and whose heart is in a very good place. In a sense that most of us can only imagine, the people shown here are her family. This was made all the more clear when so many of the people you will meet in this book—Navajo and Hopi together—came to celebrate the opening of Susanne's exhibition at the Museum of Indian Arts and Culture in Santa Fe in the spring of 1988.

She knows that these ties, greater than mere friendship, are wonderful gifts, and she has reciprocated by making all her earnings from the sale of this book a gift to Futures for Children, an Albuquerque organization devoted to the well-being of Indian children in the Southwest, to the quality of their education, the health of their communities, and the continuing vigor of their ways of life.

Whole-heartedly, then, I commend this book to you.

Robert Redford

INTRODUCTION

In the late 1960s, the United States Information Agency sent me on assignment to Arizona. I was to photograph the newly opened, Navajo-run school at Rough Rock on the Navajo Reservation for the magazine *America,* which is circulated in the Soviet Union. I was stunned. I simply was unaware that such a culture, so private, so different from mine, existed in our midst.

One thing led to another, and for a bit more than two decades I have been honored to spend a good deal of time among both the Hopi and the Navajo people who inhabit a vast region in northern Arizona and New Mexico. As a photographer, I spent most of that time with my cameras in their bag. I have herded sheep, helped around various houses, run a lot of errands. I've done a lot of knitting.

In each case, it took a long time before these private people felt comfortable enough with a white person in their midst to be themselves—still longer until they were willing to be photographed without posing. Over the years, their friendship has become too dear to be described in words.

I am aware that a book that interleaves photographs from the two tribes might be criticized as sentimental: the politically inclined might say that it ignores the only important matter, the land dispute; the

1

2 anthropologically inclined might complain that the two tribes have little, if anything, in common. But this book simply is not about tribal politics. If it is "about" anything, it is a portrayal of some people who are Navajo and some people who are Hopi and the commonality of some aspects of their lives.

A Navajo planner and friend, Rodger Boyd, was talking about this recently. He told me of a time when he was young and had the task of driving his uncle to Gallup where Rodger's mother, the uncle's sister, was in the hospital. But first the uncle wanted to stop off at Second Mesa on the Hopi Reservation. There, the two Navajos visited a Hopi medicineman who readily agreed to go to the hospital with them and perform a special ceremony for Rodger's mother.

"And," Rodger said, "this Hopi medicineman spoke *Navajo*. I've never forgotten it. It blew my mind. Of course, over the centuries, there has been some hostility between us. But I think people, especially outsiders, tend and even like to let the old hostilities turn into myth, a myth that feeds on itself. In today's age, with all of the troubles and problems in the outside world, I think the Hopi and Navajo are finding that we have more in common than our history would suggest."

I have tried to photograph people the way I feel they see themselves, rather than the way an outsider might *want* to see them. I try to see people as individual human beings—not as symbols or statements for a busy, sometimes uncaring, sometimes curious world. This book is a result of the generosity of these friends over the years, and I hope it will be taken by them as a sign of my gratitude.

Children of the Sun

6 By custom, the door of a Navajo hogan faces the direction of the dawn.

The Hopi say: Take the breath of the new dawn and make it part of you. It will give you strength.

Two peoples, two cultures—how awkward are the words. Two tribes inhabiting for as long as memory the high country of the American Southwest: one a race of pastoralists given to living in remote camps; the other villagers, argiculturalists—two traditions sometimes at odds but whose deities inhabit the same places.

The Hopi and Navajo abide in a land of majesty and magic where the light is new each moment and the sky opens daily, a new lesson to be learned, a new promise, like a newborn child. It is an unforgiving—and all-giving—land, a place that holds within it all the reality of a human mother.

For both the Hopi and Navajo, it is a sacred land, a place of spirits— kachinas and holy people—a world we might call invisible if we cannot see so well.

For both, this is a temporary place in their tribal histories and plans and in their personal destinies. Here, it is a world of emergence, transcendence.

The children here grow up in the belief that they are one with nature, no more important in the scheme of things—and no less important—than a piñon pine or a fresh breeze.

The Navajo seeks to be a part of an overall harmony, without which there is sickness and despair. A Hopi is always reminded that he or she is part of an eternal cycle, just like a corn plant.

Whether they tend flocks or cornfields, write government documents or operate a dragline, this world-view is always present, always possible, so ingrained in the mind, so inseparable from the daily round of play and work, there is no way to distinguish life from religion.

14   Surrounded and cajoled into life by voices
that are as quiet as the wind
exploring the intimate geometry
of rock and sand, anchored in
an initially bewildering world by
the faces of their clanswomen
and clansmen, taught through
the device of endless stories,
the children know just who they
are and know that they belong
just here, just now.

16 About three weeks after its birth, a Hopi
baby is named. Its paternal
aunts gather before dawn and
offer various clan names for the
child. Its hair is ritually washed
and its grandmother takes it,
and its ear of Mother Corn,
outside to be introduced to its
father, the Sun.

She will say: You will enjoy life into old age.
Never will you experience any
infirmity whatsoever until you
pass away in your sleep as an
old man/woman. And this shall
be your name...

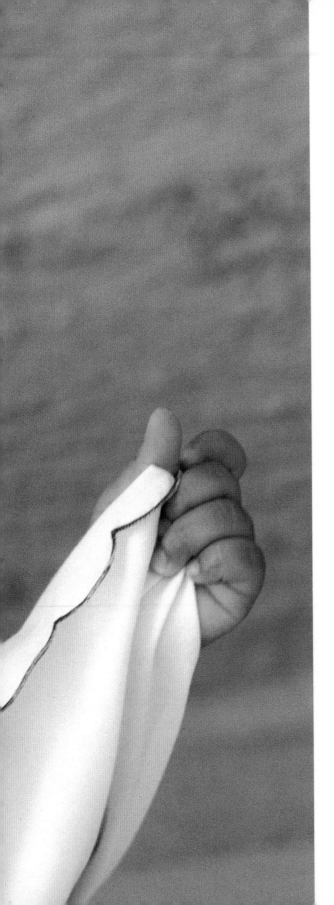

A Navajo cradleboard is made of cedar wood and used for generations. Soft cedar shavings were formerly used as an absorbent pad. The leaves of cedar are collected for making offerings, to bless people and homes, and to protect from evil. "Cedar is a protection way," a Navajo friend, Marie Saltclah from Crystal, told me, "and the cedar wood of a cradleboard keeps the baby's mind together, keeps it safe. When a baby is in its cradleboard, it is holy. We keep the cradleboard for generations. It's sacred. Though as a matter of fact," she giggled, "I don't know where ours is right now. We'll find it when it's needed."

Here, as in any coherent society, children are honored. Young people are respected as human beings, as one tribal elder said, who will come into their own at their own time.

Has a Hopi kachina ceremony ever taken place in a plaza without little kids swirling around and vanishing like small eddies of wind, a celebrated part of the day's purpose? And they are dignified as well by being part of the family's survival plan. Navajo kids herd sheep. Hopi kids learn early to help pick ears of corn.

I knew a Navajo girl, a pre-schooler, who was solely responsible in her family's camp for nursing her bedridden grandmother. Fetching food, changing diapers— already a part of the endless gyre of give-and-take in a world where a fine-tuned reciprocity is the bedrock of life and where a smile is taken to be sacred.

They grow up in two worlds now, these children, of necessity. One is the ancient world of spirits, harmony with the land, and the strength of family ties. The other is a world of television and computers, of a new global intimacy where old stories, old truths, may seem hard-pressed to account for the fruits of science and technology. An impinging society that often seems as fragmented as old potsherds scattered on the land.

One day, a Hopi pointed to the clouds rising over San Francisco Peaks. "I know how the meteorologists explain those clouds. I understand that. But I also know those clouds are the kachinas, rehearsing how to bring rain." A Navajo medicineman once took me in his truck and showed me the footprints of the holy people etched in hard rock near a canyon a few miles from Tsaile.

2 4   I have felt welcome—in particular and always first—by children.

On first visiting a remote Navajo camp, one feels a complete aloneness. For me this soon became an appreciation of space and quiet, then of the connection with the children who would translate, advise, play with my cameras.

Sometimes during my visits I became depressed that I was a photographer, that I walked with the mechanical inventions of the twentieth century slung over my shoulder, and that I could, so casually and whenever I wished, fly in and out of the lives of people of whom I had grown fond. Who, I wondered, was the nomad?

About half of all living Hopis and Navajos
are under the age of eighteen.
That's nearly 100,000 young
people—what economists like
to call "a resource."

Precious cargo indeed, each charged by
circumstance with the unim-
aginable human goal of being
bi-cultural, of reconciling within
their individual souls the opposite perceptions of the universe
and its use.

26 A Navajo tribal official told me once: "Sure, we want computers. We would like a PC in every hogan. It's just we want those computers programmed to think Navajo."

A Hopi leader said: "We want to find a way of adapting an older traditional lifeway to modern life so that we can intertwine the two without losing the good things of either, and that's going to be the new way of life in the future for us and our children."

And at a high school graduation not long ago, the students bedecked in mortarboards and robes, a tribal leader, speaking from a long history of migration, of hardship and hard work, of tradition and prayer and emergence, had this to say: "If you can imagine it, you can believe it. If you can dream it, you can make it happen."

Mother Corn

30   Hopi corn is law, meaning: To grow corn is
            to know how to behave, to know
            the nature of human life and its
            purpose in the scheme of
            things. For the scheme of things
            is embodied in the nurturing
            and use, the variety and color,
            of the ears of corn that arise
            from the earth.

To commit oneself, one's lineage, to grow-
            ing corn in a place that receives
            but a few inches of rain or snow
            each year, and to do so in dry
            washes without irrigation or
            more recent technologies, but
            only with old knowledge embed-
            ded in magical digging sticks, is
            an utmost act of faith.

32

Faith that only carelessness, or a failure of will or of generosity of spirit, could turn the earth against you and your children.

The seeds are placed in a soft, moist place under the sand and the plant is born, to be sung to and treated with cheerfulness like a child. Carefully tended, it grows. "It's not enough," Linda Quavehema told me once, "for Alonzo to pray for the corn out in the fields. I have to pray too, from here. We must be together in these prayers or they won't work."

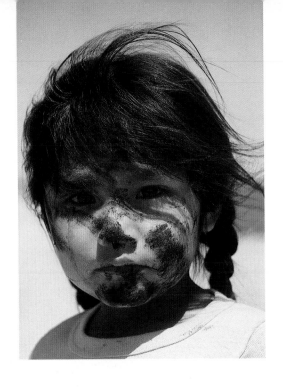

34

Ravens, locusts, other pests take their toll on new ears. It is a profane world we live in. Some of the leaves bend and touch the ground, needing its support like old people with canes.

The leaves of the corn plants will wilt, close up, in the hot sun of June and July. With the appearance of clouds, the leaves unfurl in anticipation. With even the lightest rain, the plants—as if by magic—rejuvenate and are ready to produce their own children.

Eventually the mature ears are picked. The farmer pushes the old stalks over. Their job is done. They can rest and become again part of the earth. The same Hopi word stands for the spent corn stalk and the spent human body.

Of course, there is room in all this for simple good fun. When it comes time to pick the sweet corn, some ears may have black goo on them, the result of a disease called corn smut. The trick is to attack someone and smear the goo on your companions' faces before they get you. It is also a good excuse to chase a pretty girl out of sight for a while.

So corn is the human life span. It is also the history of the gathering of the clans to the Hopi mesas from the four directions, an inward migration to the center of the world. "Oh yes, we came from down around Winslow," said a Hopi friend, as though it had occurred within his lifetime, not six hundred years ago.

Yellow corn is northwest, blue southwest, white northeast, red southeast. The corn is not a reminder of these old treks. It *is* the treks, as present a reality and as pregnant with meaning as if they had occurred within a current lifetime.

Upon emerging into this world from below, the Hopi were offered several kinds of corn—plump red ears, long white ones, short blue ones. The long ears promised a life of material comfort, but the Hopis chose the short blue corn, thus opting for lives of difficult labor but also an existence that would survive into the next world.

Besides its many meanings, I can attest that however they prepare it, few things taste better than Hopi corn.

Roasted, boiled, dried, ground into meal
and made into piki bread,
stacked and dried for later use,
prepared and kept countless
ways, corn is sustenance of
body and soul, a necessary
ingredient in ritual after ritual,
itself a prayer.

Corn meal feeds and pleases the Hopi
spirits. Likewise, corn pollen is
used in many Navajo bless-
ings, be it of the dawn or of a
healing implement.

Sheep and Weaving

The sheep—as mutton, as wool, as wealth, and as ingredient in healing ceremonies—bespeaks the Navajo life span and duty, the attention to important details of the earth and its seasons, as richly and completely as does the Hopi planter's corn.

43

If a young shepherd's attention wanders,
or an old one's energy flags,
there is the "rez dog," performing what must be one of its
most ancient tasks in return for
a living free from the hunt,
intuitively given to rounding
things up and moving them
along, a necessary busybody.

Once on a dirt road in the middle of nowhere, I saw a full school bus stop. A young sheepdog, maybe twelve weeks old, had diverted from its herd and circled the bus, rounding it up. The driver, a Navajo, and the children understood and patiently paused while this useful citizen learned its trade. Once satisfied that the bus was under control, the puppy went back to bossing the sheep.

48 Spider Woman sang and spun the Hopi world into being and saved many a Hopi from tragedy and failure. And she instructed Navajo women to weave on a loom, which Spider Man told them how to make. The cross-poles were made of sky and earth, the warp sticks of sun rays, the healds of rock crystal and sheet lightning.

Weaving begins with the shearing of sheep in spring, one at a time, by hand—the back, shoulders, and hips all in one piece, which is then folded and tied. It begins also out in the land with the gathering of lichens, cedar, and a host of other well-known plants that will dye the wool just as the sun dyes the puffy clouds of an afternoon. In the hours of foraging, the first of a specific dye plant encountered is blessed and left to grow and multiply.

The weaver takes the new wool bundles inside, cards them, and rolls them up into roving, to be spun and put in skeins. These are taken outside and boiled with the dyes. But before this step, a complete design has emerged in the weaver's mind's eye of the rug she will create.

Once dyed, the wool is washed and hung to dry with flat stones that make it straight. Then, with the help of children's outstretched arms, it is wound into balls.

A Navajo rug may mean many things.

With tools handmade by her male relatives from specially selected wood, the long process of converting her mind's-eye image into reality on the loom begins. So engrossing is the process that the weaver weaves one thread out of the design and across the border to the edge—a road out so that her personality and accomplishment will not get trapped in her new creation, making it impossible to imagine a new design.

In the winter, when the Navajo can talk of sacred things, the children learn string games, like our "cat's cradle." A medicineman told me that the geometric patterns that result have names. The designs and the names are the same as the seven sacred constellations of stars, patterns in the sky that protect one from the evils of the night. He said these same patterns are also to be found in the traditional Navajo rug.

52   At Hopi, a different tradition prevails. It is the men who weave, and from cotton, not wool. Chiefly, they weave white robes for brides (and any female children of the bride) along with a mirror-image robe, which is the woman's shroud.

When, one day, her soul reaches the Grand Canyon, she will step on this woven robe and, like a flying carpet, it will carry her safely into her next world.

Heavy Duty

5 6   Early on, the Navajos took to the horse as
well as the sheep. The horse
was part of their strength:
indeed, a Hopi told me once,
half in jest, that if you see that
you are going to have a quarrel
with a Navajo, get him off his
horse. Otherwise, you've had it.

Traditionally, Navajos think of horses as
sacred. There is a horse chant,
which, if properly done, will
cause a free-running horse to
approach you docilely. The
chant speaks of all the different
parts of the horse. It is also sung
at the Purity Way ceremony
when girls become women.
White horses are especially
revered. I heard that in the old
days a father would tell a suitor:
"If you want to marry my
daughter, you better bring
twelve white horses."

58   When I grew up, it was the cowboys
            against the Indians (though I
            wasn't allowed to be either,
            being a girl). So I was struck by
            how many Indian children like
            to brag about being good cow-
            boys. I was struck also by the
            roughness of cowboying, the
            searing heat of the brand on
            flesh, and the violence of de-
            horning. Some people say it's
            sad that the Navajo and Hopi
            have taken up this part of white
            culture. After all, mutton
            remains the meat of choice
            among both. Cattle are raised
            chiefly for market.

6 0 But I've learned that many such outward appearances are not matters of assimilation—Navajo cowboys are not becoming part of white culture by taking up cattle-raising. Nor do they lose their identity by playing basketball, a pastime beloved on both reservations. They play basketball because they want to, raise cattle because they want to, and it doesn't change their essential way of thinking. Navajos and Hopis in pickups or business suits are still Navajos and Hopis.

It is called adaptation, not assimilation, and it is why Indian societies still exist among us. Their difference from us, and from one another, is part of the glow of the earth.

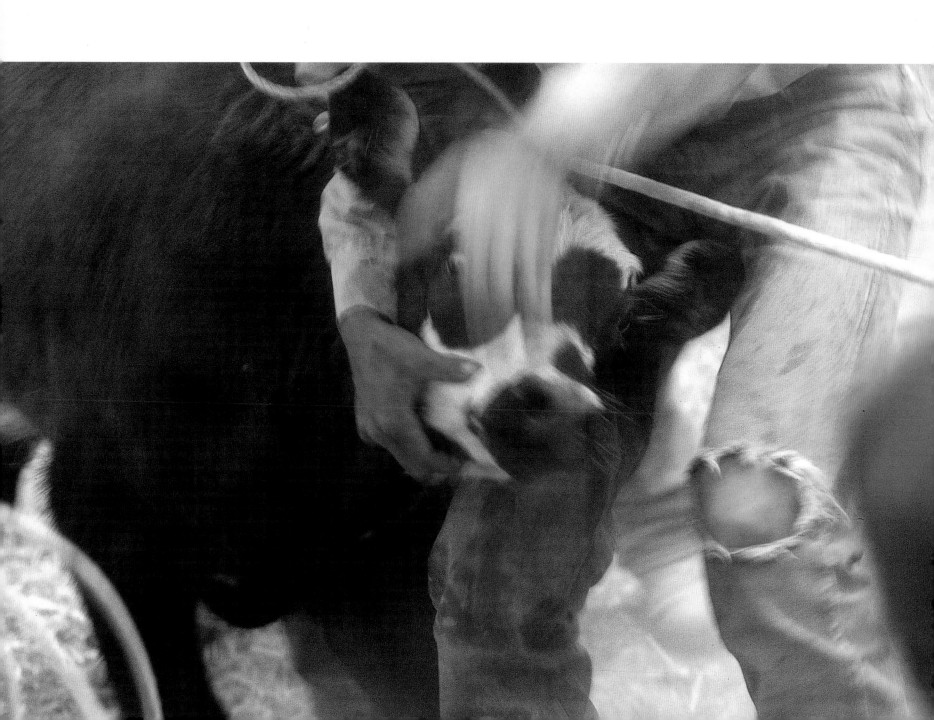

Rodger Boyd, who has a graduate degree from M.I.T., explained it this way:

"The core of a tree is always the same. Look at a cross-section of a tree. From its essential center it grows, ring by ring, a ring for a year, but the core is permanent. The rings record history—of fire, drought, flood—and how the tree managed these events. But in our core, we are always Navajo, regardless of the events written in the rings or the appearance of our bark."

Still, there is no sense in romanticizing cowboying. Working with cattle is rough on both the men and the cattle. It reminds me that there is a dark side to life. For everything good in life, there is the opposite. It is steering a course among these forces, this reality, that is the challenge of a life.

6 4

Rodeos and county fairs are common elements of rural life in the West, and the Navajos have taken these on as well and made them their own. A few decades ago, if a Navajo went to the rodeo, he saw white cowboys performing. Now, Navajo rodeos are performed by Navajos, while the spectators number many whites.

At the annual Navajo Nation Fair, it is Navajo harvests, livestock, crafts, food, race horses that are in competition. Miss Navajo is chosen based on her knowledge of traditional culture and language, and traditional skills like making fry-bread or weaving. Country-western singers vie for attention with old Navajo songs and dances—shawl dances, ribbon dances. Some stalls sell traditional food, others Anglo food. At rodeos, there are always American flags in evidence and everyone sings the national anthem.

66 Before he goes out to hunt, a Navajo hunter will sing a prayer to the elk or the deer, thanking his quarry in advance for being available to be killed so that the hunter can sustain his life and that of his family. The Hopi act similarly. Such events are interwoven in a complex system of existence, and life simply requires the sacrifice of other lives.

Mining—coal, uranium, and other minerals—is a major factor on the reservation, and many outsiders, few of whom live on dirt floors in one-room houses, grow upset at the thought of Indian people themselves stripping Mother Earth and wrenching these things from her. An old Hopi religious leader told me once that, in his view, those minerals were put there for the people's use. And they should be used, just as we breathe the air and use the water provided by the earth.

The important thing, another commentator said, "is that we have to make it new again."

A Navajo friend said, "We have to live by closing the circle. We can go out and work in the white man's world or with the white man's tools. That doesn't mean we want to be white or anything else besides ourselves. A Navajo miner, or even a striker, doesn't think in his core like a union member in Chicago. He is simply confronting a situation at hand with the available and appropriate tools. You work in such a world in order to improve the life of your people. That's closing the circle—like the hunter's prayer. We can do this—we are strong enough to do this—because we have family in the truest sense, an extended family. We can always return to our family."

At Home

The occasional sound—the clink of the bellwether sheep, the rustle of wind through piñon pines, the shutting of a door, the rhythmic thump of the weaver's comb, even the distant whine of country music from a young person's tape deck—none of these sounds interrupt the quiet of a Navajo camp so much as they reinforce it, recognize the primal silence in such a place. A soft voice is sufficient for nearly any purpose and, even in the long pauses that mark many a conversation, there is an almost palpable sense of community, of communion.

In a Hopi house, there are often what seem extraneous events. Children running in and out. Front doors slamming. Purposeful comings and goings of men on errands, women consulting. A neighbor may be playing the music from a recent dance on a tape deck, or a television set may be playing a soap to an empty room. All part of the bustle of village life.

7 2   Ensconced in the warmth of a Hopi household, one is always aware that
the farmer's life in this dry land
calls for endless labor and daily
prayer by the whole family to
the spirits of plants and rain. I
rarely went to a Hopi home
without being asked to share
their hard-won harvest. It is as if
there were a direct line from the
spirits to whom they pray to
their natural generosity.

When water is scarce, as it is in most Navajo camps as well as several Hopi villages, even a simple task like washing dishes becomes complex, time-consuming. Maintaining a household in such places is difficult and the women work as hard as any man. Yet Hopi and Navajo homes, often crowded with extended family members, are in my experience always immaculately clean. Shortly after my husband Jake and I moved to a new house in New Mexico, Marie Saltclah paid us a visit. She looked at the new house room by room and said: "It's beautiful. Where's the broom?"

It was New Year's Eve when, at midnight, Navajos bless their homes with cedar smoke. That night our house was thus blessed.

Traditionally, in both tribes, a man moves into his wife's camp or village, into a home-life that may already be populated with four generations. Whether Hopi or Navajo, his children will be born into his wife's clan, which immediately gives them an even more extended family of clan aunts and uncles, a larger connectedness to their people, rivalled in the Western world only—and weakly—by the Scottish clans.

Any clan is closely related to a handful of other clans, adding yet another degree of association. When a Navajo meets another he doesn't know, his first inquiry is about clan membership. From that information, each places the other and conversation can proceed.

76 In both tribes, there is an order of clans, based largely on when they arrived in the course of emergence and history. At Hopi, the Bear Clan was first to arrive at their promised land on the mesas, and so it is from the Bear Clan that village leaders arise. Each Hopi clan has a specific function. The Bluebird Clan followed the Bear Clan and became historians. The Tobacco Clan is charged with providing natural Hopi tobacco for ceremonial purposes. The Sun Clan provides the watchers of the sun's course, by which important events are timed.

In both tribes, the clan system is the glue that holds society together.

During the time of Hopi weddings, the groom's father's house is subject to raiding. The groom's paternal clan aunts, all of whom—young and old—have a special relationship with the groom as "girlfriend," will stage one or more raids on the household, where the bride-to-be has come for four days of grinding corn and cooking, thus proving her wifely competence. Armed with mud, the aunts come and hurl insults at the bride, pointing out her inadequacy to be wife to "their" boy. She will be defended by the groom's maternal clan aunts. Everyone is pushed, shoved, and covered with mud before the attackers withdraw.

Another raiding target of these paternal aunts is the groom's father. Complaining that he has wrongly consented to let their boy marry this incompetent stranger, they punish the father by grabbing him and cutting off some of his hair, a mock scalping. If the father cannot be found, the groom's ceremonial father (godfather) is the one who gets scalped.

Traditional homes, made from available local materials, reinforce one's closeness to nature. The house itself may belong to the wife or the wife's mother, and be on land allotted to the wife's family, but land is not owned. Land, you are told, is part of the Earth Mother and cannot be owned any more than birds or clouds or trees can be owned—all those parts of nature of which a Hopi or Navajo considers himself merely one.

Increasing numbers of people in both tribes are living in nontraditional houses—in small cities like the Navajo capital, Window Rock, and off-reservation, where some own land and homes. But most agree that such a place, say, a home in Flagstaff or Phoenix, a house with a fence around it, is not complete. You can't point to where your ancestors lived, or to holy places. But people living in such circumstances can always return—to their village, to their camp—to the place where they can better achieve tranquillity and harmony.

Ceremony

All around are palpable signs of an invisible world. Figures etched in rock or painted there bespeak lives long since gone, migrations, declarations of being. Startlingly intact remains of dwellings that thrived back almost beyond memory—Hopi revere these places as the temporary homes of their clans, their ancestors, and they will visit from time to time to commune. Navajos tend to avoid them, places where there was once life but now only its opposite. There is much to pray for and many ways of praying. Here, life is at times indistinguishable from ceremony.

Every creature, every aspect of nature has its holy people, Mike Mitchell, a Navajo medicineman told me— even the stinkbug.

Sometimes you can see them, if only for an instant. They are represented, some of them, by colors: the blue sky, the evening dusk, the night—these are holy people and one prays to them. There are iron people, crystal people, then the other rocks "and such people." There are dawn people, twilight people, air, thunder, and cloud people.

One does not talk about such things in nature when they and their holy people are present. In winter, many will have left—bears, for example—so one can speak of bears in winter. The thunder people leave in winter. In winter, the snow people, the cold air people, are present—"like a day shift and a night shift."

White thunder is different. It comes in winter. Thunder in a snowstorm is startling. "Whoever is the leader of the thunder people sends white thunder back to their summer place to see what's going on. Navajos have summer and winter camps and they go check on them, just like the white thunder."

The tornado people occasionally touch the ground. "They can twist anything, even a mind." I had already learned that one mustn't let a dustdevil touch you, or your face becomes twisted. "The holy people sometimes hurt us," Mike said, "the way we sometimes hurt little ants by accident."

In a place where evil is considered an objective reality, there are good holy people and bad holy people. Navajo prayers are for protection against the latter, and almost all their ceremonies are healing ceremonies, designed to restore balance and harmony to someone who has been "infected" by evil holy people, or harmed by one's own kind. Even an event as seemingly sociable and innocent as a Squaw Dance is a means of dealing with the effects of witchcraft.

92 Navajo medicinemen are specialists. Mike Mitchell is an herbalist. Others specialize in certain ceremonies, or Ways, for specific illnesses such as epilepsy, depression, kidney problems. Such ceremonies are long and complex, taking four days, sometimes as many as nine. A nine-day ceremony can cost $6,000 or more: medicinemen are always paid for their services. There are other medicine people who only diagnose and then prescribe the necessary ceremony. Some of these diagnosticians determine the ailment while in a trancelike state during which their hands involuntarily tremble. Others use quartz crystals—looking through one or sometimes two—to see inside the body of the patient.

Hopi use crystals to bless the kachinas in the kiva, to focus on them the infinite love and wisdom of the universe. The vast panoply of Hopi kachinas is a major part of one of the most elaborate ceremonial cycles in the world, a cycle tied to the seasons of agriculture. Indeed, they are what make Hopi agriculture possible. From about the time of the winter solstice, the kachinas begin to appear in the village—a time when the land is in the icy grip of the shortest days. Early ceremonies, among other things, implore the sun to start its return trip to its summer house. Later ones are requests for timely rain.

9 4   The kachinas are the embodiment of the
cloud spirits and in that form
they are thought of as children
of the Hopi. The Hopi take
care of them, feed them with
corn meal, and let them dance
in the plazas, which they enjoy.
In return they are asked to
bring rain.

But when the kachinas revert to the form   9 5
of clouds, they are fathers of the
Hopi. Many Hopi prayers are to
these spirits, these live beings
who, like groups of people, have
chiefs. Thus, by smoking sacred
tobacco in a pipe, a Hopi sends
a message to the chiefs of the
four directions, where the cloud
spirits dwell. The smoke, which
is the prayer, vanishes up into
the atmosphere and works its
way into the homes of the
clouds, where the chiefs await
them and invite them into
their kivas.

The chiefs speak to the prayers: "Now you
sit down. Someone, somewhere
desires our presence. That is
why we have visitors. Now let us
go and approach our mortal
fathers with moisture." And so
the kachinas come, and if the
Hopi have lived their days without resentments and envy, the
rains also come.

96 Another message to these all-important spirits is the eagle. In early spring, certain priests go to eagle nests on their traditional clan lands to pray that the mother will produce a baby eagle for them. They will leave an offering—such as a feather— in an inconspicuous shrine. Later, they return and retrieve a baby, bringing it to their home or to their clan house, where it is named in the same manner as a human baby and becomes a member of the clan.

From a perch on the rooftop, it will observe, with its legendary vision, the activities of the villagers, seeing if the Hopi have lived properly and done their ceremonies well. Then, after the kachinas have left for their winter home in the San Francisco Peaks, the eagle is sent home to inform the rain spirits that they should approach the Hopi fields. The eagle's primary feathers become a lasting part of the village's ceremonial paraphernalia, and its down feathers are made into prayer offerings called *pahos*, which are used to bless homes and pickups and are placed in shrines as yet further prayers to the chiefs of the four directions.

100   Not all ceremonies are so fraught with import for survival. The social dances of the Hopi, where males and females join to dance in the plazas, have a religious significance to be sure, and are taken seriously. But they have other purposes. Many celebrate other tribes, such as the Navajo Dance, where the dancers wear costumes approximating the traditional dress of their neighbors. "Maybe it's to celebrate us," said a Navajo friend good-naturedly, "but it's also to poke fun at us."

At pow-wows and fairs, there is always dancing, celebrations of one's Indianness. It may be difficult to understand for some people whose lives are less full of formal ritual and ceremonial form, but here ceremony is not only a way of survival, it is fun, a major source of entertainment.

The Most Beautiful People

"I always felt that everything is alive," said 105
Dextra Quotskuyva, a Hopi pot-
ter. "There's a lot of rocks out
there. They all seem to be in the
right place." She went on to talk
about how people sometimes
grow distant, out of place. "But
when we get together, we're all
one, really."

106 "Every individual," said former Navajo
tribal chairman Peterson Zah,
"has a determination, a desire,
a burning desire deep in his
heart, and I'm sure that if every
person can search for that,
and reach for that, they will be
successful in whatever they
decide to do."

Abbott Sekaquaptewa, former tribal chairman of the Hopi, has fought
staunchly for the rights of his
people over the years. Like
leaders of both tribes, he has
been in the thick of the contro-
versies that have divided the
two politically. Recently he said:
"This may seem odd coming
from me, but somewhere the
healing process must begin.
We have our differences, but
we have so much to celebrate
together—our strength, our
beauty, our aspirations for our
children. Their children are
ours, ours are theirs. You only
have to look to see that the Hopi
and the Navajo are the two most
beautiful people in the world."

Where my kindred dwell
Near the red rock house
There I will wander.
I am the Dawn Boy,
Child of the White Corn.
On the trail of the pollen of dawn
I am wandering.
Where the dark rain cloud
Hangs low before the door
I am wandering.
In the house of long life
I will wander.
In the house of happiness
I will wander.
With beauty before me
I will wander.
With beauty behind me
I will wander.
With beauty above me
I will wander.
With beauty below me
I will wander.
In old age traveling
On the trail of beauty
I will wander.
It shall be finished in beauty.

—SONG OF DAWN BOY
   from the Navajo Night Chant

AFTERWORD

My wife Susanne is a most peculiar person. A photographer, she shies away from a camera pointed at *her* the way a young horse shies from a saddle. An outgoing person, she is drawn as a photographer to private people, like those in this book, or the watermen of Chesapeake Bay, or the backwoods folk of Harlan County, Kentucky. A grandmother, she seems eternally youthful, happy to dangle over a three-hundred-foot cliff to photograph an eaglet in its nest, but stricken with terror at the thought of using a flash in someone's home—or anywhere else, for that matter. As a result, she is what I call a human tripod. Some of the photographs in this book were taken at one-quarter of a second. Leaving a lens open that long is something like forty-five seconds of dead time on television. No one does it. But Susanne resolved that there would be no artificial lighting, no set-ups, no re-enactments in her photography of the Hopi and Navajo. So she has had to make the best of noon's glare in the mile-high Southwest, as well as the dark of homes lit often with only a fire.

She wouldn't dream of talking about her accomplishments, so I frankly insisted on writing this afterword: my bias is evident, but I also know who I am talking about.

Back in the 1960s, she was a single mother with three little daughters—Lindsey, Sally, and Kendall—and she had a job as a photo editor with the U.S. Information Agency, working for a genius named Lee Battaglia. A photographer, Paul Conklin, gave her a teen-aged, beat-up Nikon and the two men gave her encouragement to try it. With what amounts to a shrug, and without the slightest notion of the optical system of a camera, she began. Before too many months had gone by, she was a full-time free-lance photographer (and still a mother) and David Brower of Friends of the Earth almost literally stole from the U.S. mails some of her photographs of Navajo people that were on their way to an author for possible use in his book. The result of all this was *Song of the Earth Spirit,* Friends of the Earth's first book about people instead of landscapes. It was a portrait of traditional life among one Navajo family who lived in a remote part of the reservation around Rough Rock and up on Black Mesa. It was published in 1972 by McGraw-Hill and, in paperback, by Ballantine. It is now sold out, a collector's item. We have two copies left, both looking a bit beat-up, and people touch them only after putting down an exorbitant bond.

After that book, things changed quite a

bit. Among other things, Susanne married me and that added three more daughters to her quill—Dana, Lea, and Brooke. She had taken to bringing a daughter or two to the Navajo Reservation on her photographic trips, not to prove that she was really a mother with a family but because she avidly wanted their company. By now, all six have been part of these sojourns.

Then, the founder of Futures for Children, Richard P. Saunders, gave a copy of her book to Hopi tribal chairman Abbott Sekaquaptewa. He has never denied my allegation that he thought: if this lady can take such nice pictures of Navajos, think what she might do with us noble Hopi people. In any event, in 1974 with me in innocent tow, she began work on a book about the Hopi. In 1982, twenty-eight visits later, many accomplished through the generosity of the National Geographic Society and the patience of NGS's Bob Gilka and Lillian Davidson, the book *Hopi* was published by Harry N. Abrams, Inc., simultaneously with an article in *National Geographic.*

In the interim, the Smithsonian's National Museum of Natural History had devoted half its rotunda space to a series of Susanne's black-and-white photographs of Indian people—Kwakiutl and Miccosukkee

as well as Navajo and Hopi.

Shortly after *Hopi* was published, there was a congressional reception for the tribal chairmen of the two tribes. The Hopi, Ivan Sidney, presented a copy of the book to the Navajo, Peterson Zah, who went off in a corner and carefully looked at every photograph. Then he came up to Susanne and said, "We want one of these, but bigger." (The Hopi book weighs eight and one-half pounds.) Susanne, again with me in tow, is working on a book about the Navajo.

An old friend, Judith Nies of Boston, decided that Susanne's light was being kept under a bushel by her own reluctance to promote herself, and announced that she was going to produce an exhibit of the best of Susanne's Hopi and Navajo work. Judy went to work, and in 1984, an exhibition called *Spirit World* and consisting of fifty color photographs opened at the oldest museum in the United States, the Peabody Museum of Salem, Massachusetts. Subsequently, it appeared in the Arco Building in Los Angeles, sponsored by the Southwest Museum, then at the Lotus Gallery in Boston, and from there it went to the Sundance Institute in Provo, Utah. Susanne was epecially happy that a Valentine's Day wedding was scheduled to take place in the hall at Sundance where the exhibit was hung, and the bride asked that it be left up for the ceremony. From there, the exhibit went to the Museum of Indian Arts and Culture in Santa Fe, New Mexico, where it hung from Memorial Day 1988 to Labor Day (both noted Indian holidays.)

Her entire family traveled from Washington, D.C., to Santa Fe for the opening, which was also a benefit for Futures for Children, and they were able to mingle with these other families she has come into, the Hopi and Navajo people she had come to know over the years, many of whom also joined her at the opening. The three sisters *(see page iii)* arrived in full regalia and I had a sense of infinitude. The same guy was there and photographed the three sisters standing in front of a photograph of him photographing them in front of the Three Sisters formation in Monument Valley. It was that kind of day.

The exhibit has been given to Futures for Children to further its cause. (The original title has been changed to correspond to that of this book, largely because some Pueblo people near Santa Fe thought that the original title might be considered sensitive by some of their people.) For nearly two decades, Susanne has contributed her

time as a photographer to Futures, an organization located in Albuquerque and founded more than a quarter of a century ago with the goal of helping Indian children of the Southwest. Both she and I and Robert Redford, who kindly contributed the foreword to this book, serve on its board of advisors. Futures provides a sponsorship program whereby some twenty-six hundred Indian kids receive funds from individuals around the country that help them stay in school. The kids also gain a friend in the outside world. Through a vast host of volunteers on the reservations, the money—in a sense a kind of personal scholarship—gets directly through to the children.

In addition, Futures runs a leadership program for selected teen-agers and a community development program that assists the tribes in attaining some goal they have determined to be necessary—be it a playground, a library, or a fire engine. They also run seminars and workshops for small Indian businesses and seem ready to do whatever the tribes feel they need help with. So both the exhibit and the proceeds from the sale of this book belong to Futures for Children, and those who have

116 reached this point can know that they have already helped in a material way to foster the well-being of Indian children in the Southwest.

Not long ago, I asked a Hopi friend how he explained Susanne's success in the difficult business of photographing such private people. He replied: "Well, it's easy. We are pretty good at looking at someone and knowing if they are sincere." I'll buy that, but he failed to mention a few other qualities.

Patience is one. Years ago, the USIA needed a photograph of then Navajo chairman Peter MacDonald. The chairman said to meet him on Monday at four o'clock in the afternoon. Susanne flew out from Washington for the appointment, only to find that the chairman was at that very moment back in Washington. He was to return the next day, so Susanne waited, and began knitting a sweater. It was Friday when Mr. MacDonald returned to Window Rock and, at about seven o'clock in the evening, said Susanne could have five minutes; he met her outside by the amazing rock formation that gives the town its name. It was getting dark. Clad in a miniskirt (the fashion at the time) and desperate to make an interesting picture, she flung herself on the ground before the chairman and ran off as many frames with a 20-millimeter lens as he would tolerate. He was sufficiently diplomatic not to let his jaw drop until after the session.

Another attribute is humility. At the opening in Santa Fe, Phyllis Wittsel asked someone to take a picture of Susanne and her in front of her photograph (see page 111). Just then, a Futures for Children sponsor, singer Olivia Newton-John, came up and Susanne introduced her to Phyllis, who immediately asked Susanne to photograph her and Olivia in front of her picture.

One of Susanne's techniques on meeting new people is to give a camera to a child and let him or her play around with it. To this day, she is in a state of bemused uncertainty over the possibility that perhaps one of the best photographs she ever produced (a black-and-white of a Navajo grandmother) was taken by five-year-old Charlene Begay in 1968.

A final note. This knitting business has insidious effects, though Susanne has three grandsons now—Zack, Tyson, and Kenny—to knit for. We have a room full of yarn. She got interested in spinning and I got her a spinning wheel. Now that we are spending more time with the Navajo, I'm suspicious that she will put her cameras back in the bag and learn to weave. And I'll have to learn how to build a loom. But if it wasn't worth it, we wouldn't have moved from the East Coast to New Mexico to be closer to all this and to the people listed below who have befriended us, and taught us, and made this book.

Jake Page

The Ami family: Norma, Janis, Doris, Renee, Boom-Boom, Skipper and Kelly; Bruce Andresen; Wilson Aronilth Jr.; Claudine Arthur; Harris Arthur; Charlene and Jerry Begay; David Begay; Mary Begay; Nathan Begay; Pat and Peter Belleto; Regina Bia; Vivian Bia and Marcus Hardy; Lew Binford; Geraldine, Malcolm, Stephen and Brittany Blackgoat; Lisa and Paul Bohannan; Sam Boone Sr.; Rodger Boyd; Jackie Bralove; Bob Breunig; Randy Brooks; Pat Burke; Claudia Caboni; Marlene, Douglas, Sheena, Alissia, Pauline, and Alexie Clark; Irene, Jimmie, Virgil, Julie, Kayla, Klaton, Kristen, Victor, Evelynia, Aaron, Nicole, Teresa, Michael, Jared, Michael II, Fitzgerald, Ferlin, Kari and Judy Clark; Nellie Coho; Mary, Bennie, Pablita, Benelda and Yvette Cohoe; Margaret and Victor Coochwytewa; Jack Cooka; Ted, Casey, Kate and Alexis Danson; Sandra,

Olivia and Philbert Dennis; Jeannette Deschenie.

Pat Ferrero; Joanne Fischer; Ruth, Ken, Michele and Chris Frazier; Miloy and Ned Hall; the Halvorsons; Glennibah Hardy; Hazel and Joe Hardy; Marjorie, Olinda, Marchelle, Rae Lynn and Raymond Hardy; Martha Harrison and family; Carl Hoffman; Brannon Holtsoi; Martha and Gene Jackson; Stephanie and Dean Jackson; David Jenney; Jessie, Woody, and their kids; Alvin and Betty Josephy; Elda and Valjean Joshevema; Valjean Joshevema Jr.; Lula and Alonzo Joshongva; Michael Kabotie; Lovetta Kescolli; Bertha and Emery Kinale; Fred, Kevin, Erick, and Michael Kootswatewa; Allison Lewis; Sandra and Roy B. Lewis; Anna Lomaquahu; Starlie Lomayaktewa; Susan McDonald; Bruce McElfresh; Richard Mike; Robbie Miller; Mike Mitchell; Bob Morton; Nancy Nahpi, Edwin Choyou, Zelda, Kris, Brian and Evan Silas; Frances, Dan, Arlo, Mikey and Mana Namingha; Andrew Natonabah Sr.; Bert Puhuyestewa; The Quavehema family: Linda, Alonzo, Darlene, Raleigh, Charisse, Debbie, Linda May, Rob, Jan, Dotson, Wilson, Philbert, Moewi, Phillip, Phyllis, and Patrice.

Robert Redford; Marie and Waleste Saltclah; Richard P. Saunders; Alfreda, Alph, Scott, Charlie and Tara Secakuku; Susan,

118   Kim, Debbie, Bonnie, Joanne and Caralee
Secakuku; Ferrell Secakuku; Dorothy
Secakuku; Abbott Sekaquaptewa; Helen
Sekaquaptewa; Emory Sekaquaptewa;
Eugene Sekaquaptewa; Marlene
Sekaquaptewa: Phillip, Caroline, and Wayne
Perry Sekaquaptewa; William Shepard;
Brendan Sheridan; Anna Mae Silas and
Milland Lomakema; Madonna Slinkey; Al
Slinkey; Josephine Slinkey and Hazel Yazza
and Inez Housewood; Theodora and Michael
Sockyma; Nancy Stone;the Staff of Futures
for Children; Jessie Talaswaima; Fannie, Ben,
Janet, Marty, and Karen Thompson; Polly
and Dan Tsosie; Peter Whiteley; Mary,
Benjamin, Jolene, Natasha, Derek and
Dwayne Wilson; Phyllis, Kevin, and Eric
Witsell; Lillian Yaiva; and Peterson Zah.

   And in memory of Wilson Clark; Chavez
P. Coho; Toby Frazier; Alfred Joshongva;
Fred Kabotie; Viets Lomahaftewa; Percy
Lomaquahu; Jim Page; Dorothy Saunders,
and Terrance Talaswaima.

THE PHOTOGRAPHS

36. Hopi woman making piki bread, Shipaulovi.

37. Hopi cornfield.

38. Pickup-full of sweet corn at dawn, Hopi Reservation.

39. Hopi girl with ground corn meal.

40-41. Herding sheep near Rough Rock. Navajo Reservation.

42. Irene Clark's sheep at Crystal. Navajo.

43. Goats and sheep, Black Mesa. Navajo Reservation.

44-45. Navajo boy with family sheep, near Crystal.

45. Rez dog. Navajo Reservation.

46. Navajo girl with baby goat near Lukachukai.

47. Jessie Cabonie with baby goat near Rough Rock. Navajo.

48. Navajo weaver near Blue Gap on Black Mesa.

49. *Above:* Lichens and Navajo wool dyed with lichens. *Below:* Navajo grandmother Glennibah Hardy at loom, Crystal.

50. Navajo weaver Glennibah Hardy at home in Crystal, with natural dyed yarns.

51. Portion of rug woven by Irene Clark with all natural dyes, Crystal. Navajo.

52. Hopi bride and daughter after Home Dance, Kykotsmovi.

53. Alfred Joshongva weaving cotton sash in Shungopavi. Viets Lomahaftewa watching. Hopi.

54-55. Horses near Saw Mill.

56. Navajo cowgirl Yvette Cohoe at Pine Hill.

57. Bennie Cohoe, Pine Hill. Navajo.

58-59. Leroy, Navajo cowboy, near Ramah.

60. Branding on Black Mesa. Navajo Reservation.

61. Branding near Ramah. Navajo.

62. Navajo cowboy at branding near Ramah.

63. Navajo cowboy greets niece at Cohoe family branding.

64. *Left:* Northern Navajo Fair, Shiprock, New Mexico. *Right:* Navajo rodeo-rider's boots, Window Rock Fair.

65. Riding bull, Navajo Nation Fair, Window Rock.

66. Navajo miner and dragline, Black Mesa.

67. Navajo coal workers on strike, near Yah-ta-hey, New Mexico.

68-69. Winter at Shipaulovi. Hopi.

70. Navajo girl and giant rooster at home, Rough Rock.

71. Viets Lomahaftewa and his granddaughter in Shungopavi. Hopi.

72. *Left:* Navajo woman in hogan on Black Mesa. *Right:* Hopi bread at Shipaulovi.

73. Preparing for a wedding at Shipaulovi. Hopi.

74. Hopi family preparing for corn roast, Howell Mesa.

75. Sunset and a Navajo girl.

76. Alph Secakuku, former Superintendant of BIA. Hopi.

77. Dan Namingha, artist. Hopi.

78. *Above:* Kids and winter mud, Kykotsmovi.